VISIONARY:

Making a Difference in a World that Needs YOU

Connect with Tony:

Facebook: www.facebook.com/TheVisionarySociety

Youtube: www.youtube.com/VisionarySociety

Twitter: www.twitter.com/Trogersjr

Website: www.TheVisionarySociety.com

Email: TheVisionarySocietyinfo@gmail.com

Cover art by Roland Ali Pantin

Edited by Bonita Jewel

Contents

This book is dedicated to the visionaries of our future.
May we create a better world for future generations
to come.

"Do your little bit of good where you are; it's those little bits of good put together that overwhelm the world." – Desmond Tutu

Preface:
Visionaries – The "Saviors" of our Society

Where would we be without visionaries? What would our world look like? We owe a great debt of gratitude to the visionary men and women of our past. They have shaped our history. They have transformed our world.

Erik Calonius noted in his book *Ten Steps Ahead*, "Visionaries are not only the stuff of legend. When we string them sequentially, one visionary following another we have described the arc of history." All significant advancements in any sector of our society can be traced back to a visionary with the passion and commitment to bring their vision to life.

This book is designed to create, guide and celebrate visionaries—the saviors of our society.

Introduction:
Becoming a Visionary

"Every great task that has ever been accomplished has first been merely a vision in the mind of its creator." – Theron Dumont

People such as Steve Jobs, Martin Luther King, and Oprah Winfrey are often credited as being visionaries. We put them on magazine covers, write books detailing their accomplishments and make movies depicting their lives. The title "visionary" is not synonymous with being well known, famous or revered; the people we recognize as visionaries today were visionaries long before anyone knew it.

As you'll see in the coming chapters, you don't need to be rich, famous, or a genius to be a visionary. Visionaries are common people with an uncommon desire to bring about change in the world. Consistent with the human condition, all visionaries have their own fears, insecurities, and setbacks but they don't let those things stop them.

Visionaries are marked by the seemingly callous pursuit of their goal. Each one lives by this unspoken motto: "I will no longer accept the life I've been given; I will create the life I envision."

Simply put, a visionary is anyone committed to the *process* of implementing their vision of a better future into reality. They are not mere dreamers of "pie in the sky" fantasies. They are initiators of practical and necessary change. Before we finish our journey together, you'll have a clear understanding of the particular process that a visionary utilizes, how it makes a difference, and how to better navigate your own. You, too, can be a visionary!

Who Should Read this Book?

In short, this book is created for visionaries and aspiring visionaries. It is written about visionaries, to visionaries, from a fellow visionary. If you are like me, you shun the thought of being average. You dismiss the idea that you have to accept the status quo. You want to be different. You want to contribute to society in some way. You want your life to mean something. You want to initiate change, make a difference, and leave a legacy. If any of these words resonate with you, then this book is for you!

Why I Wrote this Book

I wrote this book because you matter!

My goal is

- To help you recognize how irreplaceable and valuable you are to the world.

- To show you that being yourself is the best way to make a difference in the world.

- To equip you with the tools and strategies you need to make your vision a reality.

The Four Principles

This book comes out of a personal search for meaning and a way to contribute positively to the world, as well as a fascination with peering into the lives of others who have made a difference. Hundreds of hours of research and contemplation have led me to the conclusion that becoming a visionary is based on four learnable principles that *anyone* can apply to make a difference in the world.

Principle #1 – Discovering a Sense of Purpose

Purpose comes from a deep feeling or calling to solve a problem in the world. It is based on finding how you are best suited to serve your generation.

Principle #2 – Being Led by an Inspiring Vision

Vision flows from purpose. It is the solution to the problem you want to solve. It is a mental picture of how you want to enact change in the world.

Principle #3 – Formulating a Strategy

Your strategy is a combination of your goals, long-term plan, and daily agenda working together to fulfill your vision. This principle is about taking action and is one of the major qualities that separate a visionary from a dreamer.

Principle #4 – Communicating your Vision

Effectively communicating your vision is how you will enlist others to help you execute your plan. This principle is about inspiring others to come along on the journey with you.

***

These four principles allow ordinary men and women to do extraordinary things in the world. In the following chapters we will explore each principle and discover the practical tools needed to apply them.

A Word of Advice

There are several questions for you to answer as you progress through each chapter. In order to get the most value from this book, please take time to answer each question. The answers that these questions extract from you will prove to be invaluable in your quest of becoming a visionary.

Chapter 1:
Finding Purpose

*"He who has a big enough why
can bear any how."*
— *Friedrich Nietzsche*

Discovering a sense of purpose is the foundation of becoming a visionary. It is the driving force behind all visionary pursuits and the key to making our world a better place. The people throughout history that made a difference in the world did so because they were connected to their purpose. Purpose moves you beyond a life of mundane, repetitive activities to a life of meaning, contribution, and fulfillment.

What is Purpose?

Everyone is born uniquely crafted for purpose. In fact, you are the physical embodiment of your purpose. Your gifts, talents, interests, and specific personality traits empower you with the tools you need to fulfill your purpose. The definition of purpose can be summed up in one word—*why*. Purpose is not about what you do, it is about *why* you do what you do. It speaks to your motive or reason for action.

We are all connected in such a way that we find our greatest fulfillment in serving each other. You express your purpose through your unique form of service. Your unique service is tied to solving a problem in the world. Your potential to make a difference in the world is based on the problem you solve. The bigger the problem you solve, the bigger the potential difference you can make. Since everyone's purpose is tied to solving a problem, making a difference is not something you pursue; it is the natural result of fulfilling your purpose. We'll talk more about clearly defining your unique service in the next chapter.

Behind Purpose

Behind every purpose lies a level of discontent. Discontent with yourself, your environment or the world. The stronger your level of discontent, the stronger your passion and motivation will be to live out your purpose. Discontent is defined as being dissatisfied with one's circumstances. The kind of discontent we're referring to here is not a passing concern or interest. It is a deep conviction that goes beneath the surface and moves you to action.

Bono, the lead singer of the popular rock band U2, took a trip to Ethiopia with his wife Ali. There they worked in a feeding camp for several weeks and were shocked at what they saw. After witnessing starving children that didn't even have the strength to stand and greet him, he said, "I will not live in a world where this reality continues to be true." Bono's discontent with a problem he saw moved him to action and for over twenty years he has been one of the leading proponents for eradicating extreme poverty.

Think of discontent as the catalyst for purpose and contentment as the enemy of purpose. Being discontent is what gives you a reason to change, to grow, to reach for something better. Without it, you will simply maintain what is.

No Limit to Purpose

In our need-laden world, there is no shortage of problems to be solved; one is waiting on you! Purpose is not about doing what's popular, has the most potential financial gain, or even what seems most logical. It is about following your heart.

What kind of problem do you want to solve?

For example:

- Real estate developers solve housing problems in our society.

- Teachers solve information problems; they educate our society.

- Entrepreneurs solve unemployment problems; they create jobs and produce products that enhance our society.

- Chefs solve nourishment problems; they help provide sustenance for our society.

- Barbers and hairdressers help maintain the appearance and self-esteem of our society.

- Poets craft words in such a way that they bring enlightenment, happiness, and inspiration to our society.

- Activists are spokesman for problems; they bring awareness to issues that need to be solved in our society.

- Musicians solve entertainment problems; they provide the soundtrack to life.

There is no limit to purpose. We are designed to do what we are most capable of doing. What you have in you is critical to our society. The world needs your life-changing book, your inspiring painting, your unique invention, your athletic ability, your powerful voice, or your wonderful personality. Your passions, interests, and abilities link perfectly with a problem in the world. Stay alert to the problems you witness and how those spark your passion and imagination. This is a clear indictor of what your purpose could be.

How to Know When You Have Found Your Purpose

Purpose brings with it distinguishing characteristics that will alert you to its presence. With this list, you can determine if you've found your purpose. You can also use it to spot someone else who has found theirs.

1.   Love

The fundamental characteristic of a person who has found their purpose is that they love what they do. If you're doing something you love, an hour can seem like five minutes. If you're doing something that you don't love five minutes can feel like an hour. People who love what they do derive so much pleasure from it that their work doesn't feel like work at all.

2.   Passion

Passion is the energy or fuel you get from your purpose. It is the source of enthusiasm and makes a person resilient and determined to fulfill their purpose. Passionate people are never bored. They are usually accustomed to working late nights and early mornings on their purpose. Their passion won't let them sleep in or waste away hours accomplishing nothing toward their purpose.

3.   Meaning and Significance

People who have found their purpose know that there is value in what they do. They feel that they are being productive and that what they do is making a contribution to the world in some way.

4.   Obligation

People who have found their purpose feel a deep sense of mission. They have a deep sense that this is the task they must complete before they die. Another way to put it is that they feel a strong urge or calling to do what they are doing. This is what gives them their sense of urgency.

5.   Being in the Right Spot

People who have found their purpose feel as if they've found their place in the world, that they've found their domain. They express this feeling by making statements such as, "I was born to do this" or, "This is who I am."

6.   Self-motivation

People who have found their purpose don't need outside motivation to do it. Their primary motivation is not financial compensation, recognition, or approval from others. If those things come, they come as an added bonus; they are the icing on the cake. People who have found their purpose do it because they cannot *not* do it. It is a natural expression of who they are.

***

This list protects you from activities you may be good at, but that are not necessarily your purpose. Through repetition and focus you can become extremely good at a specific skill, yet it still might not be your purpose. This tension is most commonly seen in the workplace. The traditional workplace is filled with people skilled in solving problems that they have minimal interest in. This leads to unproductive work from unmotivated and unfulfilled employees. The reason they are unmotivated and unfulfilled is that the problem they were hired to solve doesn't tap into their purpose—the problem they were uniquely crafted to solve.

Part-time Purpose

I understand that everyone has responsibilities and commitments to adhere to. I'm not suggesting you should neglect your responsibilities and go on an impractical "search for purpose." What I am suggesting is that you shouldn't settle for less than what you can become.

You are one-of-a-kind, extremely valuable and irreplaceable to the world. Don't let your responsibilities become a scapegoat for not fulfilling your purpose. My advice is to follow in the footsteps of visionaries before you that have had to navigate this same issue. The majority of them used what I like to call "Part-time Purpose." That is, make your purpose your part-time pursuit. Use your evenings, weekends and other spare time as time for making progress toward your purpose. And when you really delve into it and discover your passion for it, you might be surprised to find just how much spare time you have!

For example

- The Wright Brothers worked as bicycle mechanics. They built the world's first practical airplane in their spare time.

- Sylvester Stallone, one of the most famous action movie stars of all time worked as a lion's den cleaner and a movie theater usher while pursuing acting gigs and writing the hit movie, Rocky, in his spare time.

This book comes out of my personal effort to maintain the responsibilities of my life and still make a difference in the world. It is a result of part-time purpose.

How I Found My Purpose

You usually discover your purpose in one of two ways.

1.   An epiphany

(an unexpected sudden revelation). This can be compared to love at first sight.

2.   A progressive revelation.

It is progressively revealed to you over time as you have different experiences and encounters throughout life. This can be compared to falling in love over time.

My own purpose was revealed to me through the latter. A friend invited me to a network marketing meeting (I had previously declined his offer several times). There happened to be a guest speaker that night. I came to the meeting not knowing what to expect (or even why I agreed to attend) but I'm glad I did.

The speaker's name was Dale Moncrief. He was energetic, young, confident, and extremely enthusiastic. I had never seen anything like it before. As he spoke, something clicked in me. It was as if my purpose was calling me and I had to make a choice. I could follow it and see where it led me or I could decline and stay in my comfort zone.

I chose to follow my curiosity and immediately joined the network marketing company, which turned out to be one of the best decisions I've ever made. Through our weekly business meetings and my new business associates, I was introduced to a variety of speakers, self-help books, and audio seminars. The more I listened to these programs and realized how much the speakers helped people improve their lives, the more I knew I wanted to do the same. I had found my purpose, and with that, the vision of what I thought was possible for me grew. I was hooked! This was a world I never knew existed. I would read for hours on end, devouring books into the wee hours of the night and listening to audio seminars in my car. This was a far cry from a guy who had never read a book from cover to cover in his life up to that point. In hindsight, I realize that while growing up I didn't read not because I couldn't, but because I didn't have a purpose that required me to. Over 600 books and 3,000 audio programs later, this is a habit I still eagerly indulge in every day. The decision to follow the gentle tug of my purpose led me directly to my purpose and changed my life forever.

There are some important points from my story I'd like to emphasize:

1.   I didn't choose my purpose; my purpose chose me.

Your purpose is not something you choose. It chooses you and you simply submit to its call. Finding your purpose is a process of discovery, not choice. You are discovering who you *already* are.

2.   I was already equipped with the tools I needed to fulfill my purpose.

Once I submitted to the call of my purpose and stayed in an environment that was conducive to its development, it awoke in me a predisposition for helping people by communicating ideas I never knew existed. Although you may have to work at refining the tools you have, the foundation of what you need to fulfill your purpose is naturally a part of who you are.

3.   The "tug" of my purpose is not unique to me.

This tug I'm speaking about can come in many different ways. It could be anger, curiosity, euphoria, a deep inner calling, or many other things. These tugs act as an inner compass saying, "GO THIS WAY." Your job is to follow it.

A Personal Process of Discovery

The process of discovering your purpose is highly personal and should be treated as such. The uncertainty you feel in the initial stages of finding your purpose is fertile ground for outside influences to derail your progress or completely stop it. Although you can solicit the help of a trusted friend or spouse to help you sort through your thoughts, it is imperative to understand two things.

1.   Nobody can tell you your purpose. It is something you have to personally discover and be content with.

2.   Your purpose can get buried under the doubts, opinions and expectations of others. Be careful who you share this precious information with until you are completely confident in your decision.

How to Find your Purpose

This exercise is to help you write a statement of purpose. A statement of purpose is a general description of your calling in life. These questions are not meant to be comprehensive; they are meant to stimulate thought and point you in the right direction.

As you write your answers, constantly ask yourself, *"How can I use this to solve a problem in the world?"* One or more of these questions will produce an answer that seems to jump off the page at you. This is not a coincidence. You may have just discovered your purpose.

1.   What people inspire you and why? Do they have a common theme? Row, ?

2.   What are you the go-to expert for among your circle of friends and family? A listening

ear? Motivation? Technology? Giving advice? Cooking? Spiritual guidance? Creativity?

3.   What kinds of movies inspire you? For example, my personal favorites are movies that display acts of courage, or someone overcoming insurmountable odds to achieve their goal.

4.   What topics do you **love** to read or do research on?

5.   What injustice makes you angry when you see or hear it happen? Your anger, closely tied with passion, is a clue to your purpose.

6.   What hurtful events or experiences in life have you overcome that you can help others overcome or avoid altogether?

7.   What kind of job or service would you be perfectly happy providing for free if you and your family had all your financial needs met?

8.   What one problem would you like to help rid the world of?

9.   Imagine writing your autobiography. What would you want it to say was your contribution to the world?

10. What kind of activities feed your energy and lift your spirits?

11. What can you do that makes time seem to disappear?

12. What comes easy to you and hard for others?

For some people there will be a recurring theme in the answers, clearly revealing what their purpose is. For others, there may be seemingly unrelated answers.

If you are the latter, put your answers in order according to how passionate you are about each thing. Start with the one that you are most passionate about and find ways to use that in the service of others. Keep going down the list of answers until one really resonates with you. The one that most resonates with you will inevitably be your purpose.

Recognizing the Value of Your Purpose

Now that you have a grasp of what your purpose is, or at least what it could be, this next exercise serves as a way to recognize and reinforce the significance of your purpose. These questions help you cultivate a sense of urgency, responsibility, obligation and contribution.

Print out your answers to these questions and read them aloud during the inevitable tough times of your journey. They will give you the push you need to persist past whatever you are going through at that time. A strong enough purpose can push through any pain.

1. Who needs you? Who will you directly help by fulfilling your purpose?

2.   Why is your cause so important to you?

3.   What will your purpose do for humanity or your sphere of influence?

4.   Why is it important that you act on your purpose NOW? Why not allow another year or two or ten to go by?

5.   What hangs in the balance? What will happen if you do nothing?

6.   How will you grow as a person by fulfilling your purpose?

7.   How will your purpose help the next generation in a positive way?

In this chapter we covered the problem you want to solve—your purpose. In the next chapter we will clearly define your solution to that problem—your unique vision.

***

Summary: Principle 1 – Discovering a Sense of Purpose

1. Discovering a sense of purpose is the foundation of becoming a visionary.

2. Your gifts, talents, interests and specific personality traits empower you with the tools you need to fulfill your purpose.

3. Finding your purpose is a process of discovery, not choice. You are discovering who you already are.

4. People who have found their purpose don't need outside motivation to pursue it.

5. Just because you are good at something does not mean you are functioning in your purpose.

Chapter 2:
What Do You See?

"A vision is not just a picture of what could be; it is an appeal to our better selves, a call to become something more." – *Rosabeth Moss Kanter*

Moving from purpose to vision is about moving from what you *feel* to what you *see*. Once you've found your purpose, your imagination and creativity are activated and you begin to form mental pictures—or visions—of how you can fulfill that purpose.

For example, let's say you *feel* your purpose is to help children. When you begin to *see* pictures in your mind about how you can help them, how you can create change, you are moving into vision. Visions are extremely inspiring because they exude possibility, hope, and change. They are a preview of what one has yet to become.

Dream or Vision?

To insure you grasp a clear understanding of what vision is, let us briefly discuss what vision is not. The words "vision" and "dream" are often used interchangeably, but in many ways they are diametrically opposed concepts. The following example will help you distinguish the two.

Imagine you have two friends. You ask them both the same question: "What would you love to do with your life?"

Your first friend enthusiastically responds, "I want to spend my life helping people!"

Your second friend equally enthusiastically responds, "I want to found a nonprofit organization committed to helping women under the age of 15 overcome self-esteem issues!"

Both statements are similar in context but the difference is obvious. Your first friend has a dream. Your second friend has a *vision*.

A dream is a vague, general statement of intent. A vision is a clear, specific, unique statement of intent. The lack of clarity and focus of a dream makes it impossible to create a logical plan for its attainment. A vision's clarity, specificity, and defined boundaries enable you to create goals, formulate a plan for its attainment, and communicate it effectively.

The old saying, "Nothing comes to a dreamer but sleep," is true. In order to act on your dreams with your eyes open, you need a clear, specific vision of the future.

Vision is Revealed in Phases

Vision is progressive. It is revealed in incremental stages over time. Do not allow the uncertainty of not knowing all the details hinder you from starting. Create your inspiring vision as far into the future as you can see, and then come back to the present and begin. As you become more aware of the specifics and uniqueness of what inspires you, your vision will grow and become more refined.

In a recent interview, international author and speaker Dr. John Demartini remarked that in the last 39 years he has updated and refined his vision statement 69 times. This practice has clearly served him well as he has accomplished great things in the world.

Fear of What You See

Fear is an ever-present enemy of progress. Left to its own devices, it will quickly choke the life from any noble pursuit. Fear strives to keep you small. To play it safe. To be average. To color inside the lines. To live within the confines of your comfort zone.

Vision is the complete opposite. It calls you to grow. To take risks. To be above average. To break rules. To move beyond the artificial boundaries of your comfort zone. This dichotomy cannot be avoided and must be sufficiently managed if you are to continue in pursuit of your vision.

You may be thinking, "How exactly do I overcome my fears? How do I stop fear from keeping me in my comfort zone?"

The antidote to fear is courage.

Courage is the ability to act *in spite* of fear, not in its absence. It is the ability to feel the fear and move forward anyway. You cultivate courage through practicing selflessness. Selflessness is putting the needs and wishes of others above your own. Fear has no place in an environment of selflessness.

For example, imagine you are extremely concerned about helping teenage kids stay away from drugs and deal with peer pressure. You've made many mistakes in your teenage years and want to help others avoid doing the same. You feel inspired to begin sharing a message of leadership, goal-setting and self-confidence at local high schools in your surrounding area. The problem is, you've always been terrified of public speaking. You violently shake and become ill at even the thought of speaking in a group setting. What do you do?

Fear says, "I can't do it. The pain of possibly being laughed at and embarrassed is too much to bear."

Selflessness says, "For the kids' sake, I have to go through with this. They need the message I have to give them."

Courage says, even as your knees shake and your stomach turns, "When do we begin?"

Understanding and internalizing this idea is absolutely critical. *The journey you're on is much bigger than yourself.* It goes back to the foundation of becoming a visionary—your purpose. Remembering what your purpose is, who it will affect, and its significance to society as a whole, will help you exemplify courage and selflessness whenever fear tries to show up.

Review the answers you wrote to the questions in chapter one. They will help re-enforce the significance of your purpose.

No Vision too Small

Being a visionary is about

- Breaking the cycle of tradition

- Being a leader

- Not accepting the status quo

- Turning your back on what is for the sake of what could be

How this is expressed will be different for everyone. Creating change in the world is not left only to the visionaries with a global vision. It begins with you and radiates outward. Your vision of change does not need to be global to make a difference; it just needs to be bigger than yourself. Joseph Campbell put it perfectly when he said, "A hero is someone who has given his or her life to something bigger than one's self."

The magnitude of our society necessitates visionaries at different levels of influence. Let your vision dictate what level you play on. Is your primary focus your family? Your local community? Your state? Your country? The whole world? Each level of influence has its place and none is more significant than the other. Each piece of a puzzle is needed to make the complete puzzle possible.

The Power of Choice

The power to make a difference is the power of choice. What one person decides to do or not to do can effect an entire generation and beyond.

- One person can decide to be the first in their family to earn a college degree.

- One person can decide to break the cycle of drug addiction in their family.

- One person can decide to end generations of poverty in their family.

It takes one person with vision to be first. To see beyond what life presents as normal. To create a "new normal" for future generations. Your vision may not change global history, but it can change your personal history and there is nothing insignificant about that. Don't follow the well-worn path. Go where there is no path and leave a trail.

The Six Components of Vision

There are six fundamental components of vision. Before you go through the process of writing your personal vision, it is vital that you understand each component.

1. Clarity – A vision should be clearly stated and easily comprehendible.

2. Specific – A vision should have a specific emphasis and clearly defined boundaries.

3. Socially-oriented – Vision is not based on selfish ambition. Your vision should improve, help or enhance society in some way. We cannot erase from history the visionaries who lived lives beyond self-preservation. Depending on the scope of your vision, your focus may be geared toward people, animals or nature.

4. Solution-oriented – Every vision is a solution to a problem. It seeks to be a future solution to a present problem.

5. Unique – Like your fingerprint, your vision is totally unique. No matter where you look, you'll never come across another quite like it. There may be many people who feel called to play the same instrument as you, write a book on the same topic, or solve the same world problem, but because of your individuality, no one will go about doing those things quite like you. In short, your vision

is what distinguishes you from every other human being on earth.

For example, at my company, The Visionary Society, our purpose is to aid in the development and advancement of our world for future generations. Our vision is to build a multifaceted global platform designed to unite, encourage, inspire and equip visionaries with the tools and strategies they need to make a difference in the world. There are many different companies and individuals who are also called to this purpose. Our vision is what separates us from the pack and displays our individuality and uniqueness to the world. It will be the same for your organization, company, or personal vision.

6.   Compelling – A well-crafted vision will evoke emotion in you. It will be exciting, inspiring and sometimes even move you to tears of joy and gratitude. This "WOW" factor you get when you document your vision is a clue that this is the vision for you. Don't be surprised if others show disinterest and apathy toward your vision, particularly the people that are closest to you. This can be extremely disheartening and serve as a major psychological blow. Understand that this is one of the perils of being a visionary; it is a part of the process. Move forward despite this discouragement and boldly pursue your vision.

Writing your Personal Vision

Writing your vision is a process of introspection, documentation, and revision.

- Introspection is the process of examining your thoughts, desires, and aspirations.

- Documentation is the process of recording those thoughts, desires, and aspirations.

- Revision is the ongoing process of editing, updating, and refining what you have documented.

The following steps will help you walk through this process:

1. Get alone.
   Schedule a block of uninterrupted time dedicated to doing this exercise. Get away from all distractions. Relax. Prepare yourself to think and write.

2. Write down all your desires and aspirations related to fulfilling your purpose.
   How do you see yourself fulfilling your purpose? What are you doing? Where are you? Visualize exactly how you want to create your future. Be as detailed and specific as possible. These desires and aspirations become the vision you want to create.

3. Summarize your desires and aspirations in one concise sentence.

It may be easier to begin by summarizing your vision into three sentences. Then merge it into two sentences. And finally, create one concise sentence. Your goal is to strip away all but the heart of your desires and aspirations. Capture the core of what you envision. This becomes your personal vision statement.

Here is an example of how your vision statement can be crafted using the six components of vision. This example also shows you how one purpose statement can have many different corresponding vision statements. As I previously wrote, many different people may have the same purpose or calling, but vision will always be unique to the individual.

My Purpose – To help people live happier and more fulfilled lives.

My Vision – To become a financial adviser so that I can assist people from (your city, state) in the low-to-middle-class income range to better manage and invest their finances.

✳✳✳

My Purpose – To help people live happier and more fulfilled lives.

My Vision – To found an organization that will print and freely distribute books and pamphlets dedicated to raising awareness in (your state) about the causes and cures of the top three deadliest diseases in North America.

✳✳✳

My Purpose – To help people live happier and more fulfilled lives.

My Vision – To become a nationally known motivational speaker and author so that I can encourage and inspire young adults from all walks of life to overcome obstacles and achieve their goals.

✳✳✳

Developing a clear, concise, *and* compelling vision is hard work. This process takes time. Remember, vision is revealed in phases. Your vision statement does not need to be perfect before you begin. Consistently schedule time to review, update and edit your vision. It will evolve over time.

You may want to create something similar to what I like to call "My Vision Book." This is a document on your computer or a notebook where you keep everything pertaining to your vision. Review your purpose, vision, goals and plan *at least* every three months. This will be an invaluable tool for you.

✳✳✳

Summary:
Principle Two - Being Led by an Inspiring Vision

1. Purpose is based on what you feel; vision is based on what you see.

2. A dream and a vision are two distinctly different concepts.

3. Fear cannot grow in an environment of selflessness. Focus on the needs and wishes of others and you will conquer your fear.

4. Your vision does not need to be global to make a difference; it just needs to be bigger than yourself.

5. There are six components of vision: clarity, specific, socially-oriented, solution-oriented, unique, and compelling.

Chapter 3: Making Your Vision Real

"Our goals can only be reached through the vehicle of a plan, in which we must fervently believe, and upon which we must vigorously act. There is no other route to success." − *Stephen A. Brennen*

Your vision provides no value to society in the intangible world of your imagination. Vision must be made real—or tangible—before you and those around you can reap its benefits. You bring your vision to life with focused action. Focused action comes from a plan. Your plan is what gives substance and practical application to your vision. Without a written plan, you are merely a dreamer.

Goals Create Your Plan

Goals are the foundation of a plan. Before you can create a plan, you must know your goals. Think of your plan as a bridge from where you are to where you want to be, and your goals as the steps along that bridge. Goals can be defined as the systematic necessary steps toward the attainment of your vision. They are the *prerequisites* you must satisfy before you have the privilege of seeing your vision come to fruition.

Every destination requires different steps to get there. When you choose your goals, you are simultaneously choosing your destination. Choose your goals according to your unique vision.

Identifying Your Goals

As I said earlier, goals are the systematic necessary steps toward the attainment of your vision. What practical things do you need to do to achieve your vision? List everything that you can. Leave nothing out.

1. _____

2. _____

3. _____

4. _____

5. _____

6. _____

7. _____

8. _____

If you're having trouble writing each step to achieving your vision, don't be discouraged. Keep in mind this important point: it is an illusion to think that you must know every step before you start. You only need to see the next step to walk up a staircase. Focus on the goal in front of you and the other steps will be revealed as you go. As Richard Evans, author of *The Christmas Box*, wrote, "Everyone who got to where they are had to begin where they were."

Creating Your Plan

A plan is a written list of arranged actions necessary to achieve your vision. Take your goals from the list above and arrange them by sequence and priority; determine what has to be done first and what is most important. Next, categorize them by deadline. What needs to be completed within a year? A month? A week?

1. _____

2. _____

3. _____

4. _____

5. _____

6. _____

7. _____

8. _____

9. _____

Plans must be Flexible

Unexpected obstacles and setbacks are normal. Life has its way of not conforming to your plans and you must be able to adjust accordingly. Make the commitment that you will plan through, over, or around whatever life throws at you without losing sight of your ultimate purpose; this will guarantee your success.

One of the best examples of this concept is found in the life of two ordinary guys from Ohio named Wilbur and Orville Wright. They wanted to solve what they called "the human flight problem." Their journey to flight was one of countless plane crashes, errors in judgment, miserable weather conditions, health problems, mechanical problems, financial problems, and hundreds of hours of planning. After nine years of constantly making course corrections while staying fixed on their purpose, they eventually created the world's first practical airplane---the solution to the human flight problem.

When your plans fail, you must not give up; failure is part of the process. Adjust your course, not the destination.

Your Daily Agenda

You have now determined your goals and written down your plan. The last step in the planning process is your daily agenda. Your daily agenda is the secret to your success. It is how you will achieve your goals and accomplish your plan. Seeing your vision become a reality will require commitment. *What you are committed to will show up in your daily agenda.*

Your daily agenda is a list of scheduled activities you plan on completing *that day.* Here's a simple but effective way to make continual progress toward your vision. Each morning before you start your day, list three high-priority activities you can do that will move you closer to your vision. Make a commitment to complete these tasks before you retire at night. The power in completing these tasks lies in the compound effect of making this process a *daily* ritual. If you are at a very busy time in life or juggling work, schooling, parenting, *and* progressing in your life goals, commit to complete at *least one* high-priority activity each day.

Big achievements have always been the result of accomplishing a series of small tasks over time. Your daily agenda is the final link in the chain of everything we talked about thus far. It starts a sequence of activities that lead you directly to your ultimate purpose.

Here is how it works. As you complete your daily agenda, you are accomplishing your plan—> as you accomplish your plan, you are achieving your goals—> as you achieve your goals, you are manifesting your vision—> as you manifest your vision, you are fulfilling your purpose.

This chapter has been about one thing—taking action. Visionaries make a difference in the world because they are action-oriented people. Now that you have completed your plan, you have an actionable guide toward your vision. Remember this statement: *Good intentions, vision, and plans by themselves will not effect change in the world; they must be combined with focused, consistent, action.*

Technically, after reading the first three chapters and doing the corresponding exercises, you can be considered a visionary. But whether you are a parent, business leader, or someone with a global vision of change, you won't get far alone. You will need to enlist the help of others to make your vision a reality. This fact leads us to the fourth and last principle of becoming a visionary—communicating your vision.

Summary: Principle 3 – Formulating a Strategy

1. Your plan is what gives substance and practical application to your vision. Without a written plan, you are merely a dreamer.

2. Your goals are the prerequisites you must fulfill before you have the privilege of seeing your vision come to pass.

3. Your plan should be flexible while your ultimate purpose must remain the same. Adjust your course, not the destination.

4. What's important to you gets scheduled. Your daily agenda holds the key to the success or failure of your vision.

5. Vision combined with focused, consistent action can change the world.

Chapter 4:
Communicating Your Vision with the World

"It's not the people who are right that change the world. It's people who can communicate their definition of right to others." – Leonard Sweet

Effectively communicating vision is an unavoidable hallmark of every visionary. Visionaries such as Steve Jobs, Martin Luther King, and Barack Obama are admired for their supreme skill in this area. Vision is captured in private but it must be communicated in public to attract the necessary resources for its fulfillment.

The larger and more complex your vision, the more time, energy, and financial resources it will take to make it a reality. People will give generously to a cause they feel inspired to give to. In order to inspire them, you must answer four questions that they will undoubtedly ask.

1. **Why should I care?**

2. **What are we going to do?**

3. **How are we going to do it?**

4.   What are you doing?

The first three have to do with how you verbally communicate your vision and the last question has to do with how you nonverbally communicate your vision (which is arguably the most important).

"Why should I care?"

This question is one of purpose. Essentially, it means, "Give me a reason to care." This is where you enthusiastically and methodically state the problem you or your organization wants to solve. Focus on describing the pain this problem causes and why this must not be allowed to continue. A word of caution: don't make the mistake of assuming that because the problem is glaringly obvious to you, it is the same for those you are speaking to; most often, this is not the case.

Take your time and clearly explain the problem. Your job is to help them understand the full weight of the issue, to make them *feel* your burden. Set up the problem as a villain or enemy in your story. Introducing this antagonist gives them an opportunity to step in and be the hero as they join forces with you to solve the problem. You will need the contribution of many hands to make your vision a reality; you get hands involved by capturing hearts.

"What are we going to do?"

Now that they understand the problem you want to solve, you have created the proper context in which to share your solution to that problem—your vision. Communicating your vision is about creating and sharing a verbal picture of the future that you want to create. This verbal picture should be so vivid and rich with detail that they can literally walk through the vision with you as you explain it. Your goal as the spokesman of the vision is to communicate it in such a way that the people you are communicating to adopt your vision as their own—it becomes a shared vision.

In other words, you can no longer say, "This is my vision." It is now *"our* vision." We all have a shared responsibility in making it a reality. Shared ownership of a common vision is what mobilizes movements, inspires paradigm shifts, and creates unity among people. *When a group of passionate people rally together around a central idea, they become an unstoppable force that nothing can stop from achieving its aim.*

"How are we going to do it?"

Now that they are inspired to come along on the journey with you, it's time to share your strategy to achieve the vision. This is necessary for several reasons:

- As a leader, it is irresponsible to ask someone to follow you into the woods with no map.

- It gives people a chance to think about what their specific role will be in the implementation of the strategy.

- Seeing the roadmap makes the journey practical. It gives them confidence and motivation to move forward. It develops a collective sense of "It is possible" among the people.

- A plan makes it easier for you to attract financial support. People are more likely to invest or donate to a cause with a sound plan of execution.

- Although my advice is to completely ignore critics and naysayers, a plan is an effective weapon against people who doubt and criticize your vision.

As you can see, sharing your strategy is the next logical and necessary step in inspiring people to help you achieve your vision, but there is one more question you must answer before people will fully commit to following you.

"What are *you* doing?"

This question is about your character. It's what qualifies you for the privilege of being followed. People associate the credibility of the visionary with that of the vision. If they do not believe in your character, no matter what you say or how you say it, your vision will fall on deaf ears.

The key to being perceived with high levels of character is personifying the vision. Personifying the vision is about modeling the message; you become a physical example of what someone inspired by the vision looks like. People respect, admire, and passionately follow visionaries that wholeheartedly personify the vision they are communicating.

Mother Teresa was a perfect example of this. She felt called to help those whom she termed, "The poorest of the poor." She cared for, fed, and voluntarily lived in the slums with them day in and day out until her death. To understand her vision, you only needed to watch her for a day. This example of character is what allowed her to inspire over one thousand nuns to aid in the fulfillment of her vision. *What you do will always speak volumes more than what you say.* The way she lived is why her influence lives on even after her death.

The ultimate goal of these four questions is to create "evangelists" for your cause. Evangelistic team members are so excited and enthusiastic about being a part of the vision that they willingly tell others. This is how your vision's influence will organically grow and perpetuate itself without your direct input. The proof that you have effectively communicated the vision is revealed in how well your team can communicate it in your absence. You'll know you have succeeded when your team clearly communicates the vision through their words as well as their deeds.

Dealing with Criticism

One of the hardest realities to face is the fact that not everyone will subscribe to your particular vision of the world. Expecting everyone to do so is unrealistic and sets you up for continuous discouragement.

Vision always stands in contrast to what is. Its future-oriented nature makes it fertile ground for criticism. You must become comfortable with the fact that people will laugh at your vision, call you a dreamer, try to convince you with data that it will not work, give you a detailed account of your past failures, or ignore you all together. Again, this is to be expected and is a part of the process of achieving your vision.

When criticism comes your way, think of it as a test to prove your resolve. Do you really believe in what you see? Will you allow the critical voices around you to shrink your vision? Criticism from others makes the realization of your vision that much sweeter, not because you proved someone wrong but because you didn't allow their criticism to stop you. The sense of pride and achievement that comes from overcoming obstacles in pursuit of what you believe in is always worth the fight.

Be careful though, because sometimes the people we call naysayers are actually correct! Maybe you don't have enough finances to support the vision. Maybe you really do need more time then expected to achieve the vision. Maybe there is a hole in your strategy that was not fully examined. As visionaries, sometimes we can be so busy in the clouds that we miss what's on the ground. Don't dismiss every opinion that is contrary to your own as "criticism."

Consider two things:

- The motive of the person giving you the information

- The validity of the information they are giving you

Constructive criticism could possibly be one of the best things that ever happens to your vision. It takes a wise visionary to discern the difference between the two.

Keeping the Vision Alive

Everything long term tends to drift off course; vision is no exception. Consistently re-communicating the vision with your team is one of the primary functions of the visionary. It is a non-negotiable activity that must be adhered to if the team is to remain focused, disciplined, and consistently progressing toward the vision. Your job as visionary is to make sure the ship maintains course.

Reminding your team of what the vision is and why the vision exists will serve you in many ways:

1. The vision helps streamline activities and provides a filter through which all decisions can be made.

2. The vision provides you with a model against which you can measure your success. The original vision you set out to create is the true measure of success for your company or organization;

growing in size, popularity or profit does not necessarily mean your organization is successful.

3.   The vision keeps the team inspired. It allows them to connect meaning to seemingly mundane tasks.

4.   The vision helps maintain a culture of camaraderie. In this environment of trust, fellowship, and commitment, the team members' priority naturally shifts to the shared goals of the group.

5.   The vision will keep you productive. It guards against the natural tendency to stagnate or become comfortable in your present stage of development.

Plan time to communicate the vision to your organization on a regular basis. This practice should be woven into the fabric of every organization's existence. It is what will keep the vision an alive, fully-functioning, force of change.

Summary:
Principle 4 - Communicating Your Vision

1. Whether you are a parent, business leader, or someone with a global vision, you will need the help of others to achieve your vision.

2. People will give generously to a cause they feel inspired about. In order to inspire them, you must answer four questions: Why should I care? What are we going to do? How are we going to do it? What are you doing?

3. Visionaries that inspire people to help them have high levels of character and model the message they are communicating.

4. You must become comfortable with the fact that people will laugh at your vision. Think of criticism as a test that has come to prove your resolve.

5. Regularly re-communicating the vision to your team is imperative to its success. It is what will keep the vision alive.

Conclusion

Now that you have examined the four principles of becoming a visionary, the real work can begin. What you do from this point on will determine the difference you make and the legacy you leave. My hope is that by reading this book you now understand how valuable you are to the world and that it is possible to live a life of meaning, purpose and significance. I'll leave you with a quote that sums up the core message of this book in one simple phrase:

"Find something that inspires you and serves the world; then go dedicate your life to it!"

Appendix 1

Checklist: "Essential Skills and Qualities of a Visionary"

This checklist is provided to give you an overview of the essential skills and qualities of an effective visionary. The more skills and qualities you can check off from this list; the more likely it will be that you can achieve any vision you have set for yourself.

☑ **Persistence**

The dictionary definition of persistence is "the quality of continuing steadily despite problems or difficulties." It takes a mixture of stubbornness and faith to be persistent: stubbornness that you will not quit until you get what you want and faith that if you don't quit, you will eventually get what you want. Are you prepared to persist past obstacles and difficulties that come your way?

☑ **Patience**

In our society of instant gratification, patience is usually not one of our strong points. To the visionary, however, it is an indispensable quality to adopt. Patience is an emotional state of self-control that simply says, "I will wait my turn."

How patient are you? Do you need to work on this area of your character?

☑ **Passion**

Passion is the infectious energy that visionaries receive from their purpose. It is how they consistently pull off superhuman-like work schedules, sometimes without even being physically tired. Are you passionate about your purpose? Is your passion strong enough to keep you up late and wake you up early?

☑ **Optimistic Attitude**

Unlike a dreamer, visionaries are practical individuals. They are **realistic** optimists; they acknowledge that there will be challenges and setbacks on the road to their vision, but they hold to the belief that they can successfully navigate anything in their path. Are you a realistic optimist?

☑ **Discipline**

Everything on this list hinges on discipline. It takes discipline to integrate each of these qualities into your character. The best definition I've heard for discipline is, "Decisions dictated by a determined destiny." Are your decisions moving you away from or toward your determined destiny?

☑ Health and Vitality

When you discover how valuable you are to the world, your sense of self-worth goes up. When your self-worth increases, you begin to take better care of yourself. Among other things this includes the quality of food and drink you put into your body. Take inventory of your daily diet. Does it complement the vision you have for your life? Does it contribute to the overall mental and physical health of your body? Does it promote energy and vitality? If the answer is no, what changes do you need to implement?

☑ Selflessness

Selflessness is thinking about the needs and desires of others above your own needs and desires. Visionaries that make an impact in the world are concerned with being a solution to a problem. Is your primary focus the needs of others? Do you want to leave the world in better condition than you found it?

☑ Commitment

Life's normal trials and tribulations will thoroughly test your commitment to achieving your vision. Your commitment is proven by what you do during the tough seasons of your journey. Are you totally committed to making your vision a reality?

☑ Courage

There are no fearless human beings on earth, just courageous ones. Courage is the ability to act in spite of fear, not in its absence. Fear only has the power you give it through your conscious thoughts. Fear is faith in your enemy. Every visionary's enemy is the status quo. Practice the quality of courage. Move toward your vision in spite of the presence of fear. What do you fear about the vision you see? Will you allow it to stop you?

☑ Gratitude

Gratitude is a sincere appreciation of a person or a thing. In a world where so many people are lost without direction and believe their life has no meaning or significance, feeling a sense of gratitude that you have found your place in the world should be natural. The best way to express your gratitude is to fulfill your purpose and help people fulfill theirs along the way. Are you grateful that you have found your purpose? Who can you help to discover theirs?

☑ Teamwork

Since nothing great can be accomplished by one man, visionaries must be able to work in a team environment. When two or more people come together for the purpose of achieving a common vision, you have a team. Are you a team player? Do

you work well with people? What can you do to
become a better team member?

☑ **Focus**

Your ability to center your energies on a given
task until completion is imperative to your success.
Whether you are working on an invention, a
painting, or writing a book, make it the focal point
of your efforts. What is your primary focus at this
time? Are you completely focused on it?

☑ **Purpose**

Purpose is the foundation of becoming a visionary. Everything a visionary does is based on the
purpose he or she decides to fulfill. Purpose is the
end toward which all visionaries exist. Have you
answered the questions in chapter one on finding
your purpose? What is the purpose you have
decided to fulfill?

☑ **Vision**

Vision is a mental picture of the potential destiny
of a thing. You could say that vision is the leader
of the visionary leader; it is what guides the visionary into the future. Are you clear about the vision
you want to create? Did you use the exercise in
chapter two to craft your vision statement? Does
it inspire you?

☑ **Communication**

You must be able to communicate and persuade people of your ideas. Communicating your vision is about persuading people that the future you see is better than the present conditions around them. Can you clearly articulate your vision of the future?

☑   **Mentorship**

A mentor is a trusted teacher. Someone's advice that not only you hear, but that you also follow. It is unlikely that you have all the knowledge and skills you need to achieve your vision. Locating competent mentorship in areas outside of your expertise will be critical to your success. Identify and document the key areas you will need mentorship in then seek counsel in these areas accordingly. A mentor can be someone that you meet with personally, or someone that mentors you from a far such as through the internet or a book. What are the key areas you need assistance in? Have you located quality mentors to help you?

Recommended Resources

Using the Internet to get your message out

1. *Crush It* (book) By Gary Vaynerchuk

2. *Jab jab jab Right hook* (book) by Gary Vaynerchuk

3. *The millionaire messenger* (book) by Brendan Burchard

4. The expert's academy (online course) by Brendan Burchard www.ExpertsAcademy.com

Leadership

1. *21 indispensable laws of leadership* (book) By John Maxwell

2. *Winning with people* (book) By John Maxwell

3. *17 indisputable laws of teamwork* (book) By John Maxwell

4. *The spirit of leadership* (book) by Myles Munroe

5.   *Passing it on* (book) By Myles Munroe

6.   *Demartini on leadership* (Audio Set) By John Demartini www.DrDemartini.com

Entrepreneurship

1.   *Knockout entrepreneur* (book) By George Foreman

2.   Business Mastery (Audio Set) By John Demartini www.DrDemartini.com

3.   *How to get rich* (book) By Felix Dennis

4.   *The Midas touch* (book) by Robert Kiyosaki and Donald Trump

Health

1.   *The 7 pillars of health* (Book) By Don Colbert

Public Speaking

1.   Speaking on your feet (Audio Set) By Brian Tracy www.BrianTracy.com

2.   Communicate with power (Audio Set) By Brian Tracy www.BrianTracy.com

3.   *Speak To Win* (book) By Brian Tracy

4. The Expert's Academy (online course) By Brendan Burchard

General Success

1. *No Excuses: The power of self-discipline* (book) By Brian Tracy

2. *Goals* (book) By Brian Tracy

3. *The Law of Success* (2008 edition book) By Napoleon Hill

Inventors

1. *The big idea* (book) By Donny Deutsch

2. *One simple idea* (book) By Stephen Key

Acknowledgements

I would like to express sincere thanks to the many people who have helped me along my journey thus far. Each of you has played an integral part in the development and refinement of the person I am today. To my father, Tony Rogers Sr. who always told me to be a leader, not a follower, and that he was proud of me. Thank you for being there for me throughout my life.

To my mother, Sondra Rogers, who always exemplified courage and ambition in pursuit of her goals. Thank you for showing me that through hard work and dedication, there is no limit to what I can do.

To my twin sister, Tonisha Rogers, a true trailblazer who has never followed the crowd. Thank you for being yourself.

To my best friend, Lakecia Mcgraw, for your many encouraging words, support and enthusiasm for this project. Thank you for being a listening ear even at three in the morning. This project would not have been possible without you.

To my virtual mentors: Brian Tracy, Myles Munroe, Mike Murdock, John Demartini, Alexander Graham Bell, Jim Rohn, Gary Vaynerchuk, Brendan Burchard, and Jesus Christ. You all taught me that a life of service is a life worth living. Thank you for living lives in pursuit of purpose.

I could write an entire book thanking people who have helped me and positively influenced me throughout my life. Others include Shaunte Brewer, Julie Hargis, Desjuan Brown, Dale Moncrief, Julio Alvarado Jr., Emma Mays, Clarence Mays Jr., Eric Thomas, Joe Vagnone, Bobby Bogan Jr. and many more. From the bottom of my heart, thank you all!!

Made in the USA
San Bernardino, CA
09 June 2015